Ehdaro:
Zhatındee Kų́ę́ gots'ęh denelı̨a dų̨ meghayé, łıé dzę meghǫ́t'ǫh

BIG POINT: A DAY IN THE LIFE OF A
FOUR YEAR OLD DENE BOY

For all the little ones,

may you have dreams,

memories of your grandmas

and your grandpas.

Mahsi.

Sharing stories can capture our imagination and draw us into a current or historic moment, and a glimpse into what is most important in our relationships with one another and the land that sustains us. This book invites us to journey and reflect on a lovely childhood memory and relationship that carries throughout time.

Over the past five years, TakingITGlobal's Connected North program has collaborated with Deh Gáh school in Fort Providence, Northwest Territories as one of our community partners. I have immensely enjoyed my visits to Fort Providence, and the warmth and friendship extended by Karalyn Menicoche, an emerging leader from the community, and her family.

Our team is grateful for the opportunity to collaborate with Chief Joachim Bonnetrouge to develop this story about his life as a young child before he was taken to residential school. As we reflect on our roles in the process of intergenerational healing and community-building, what inspires me most about the story that unfolds in this book is the importance of our shared responsibility to care for our families and the land, water and air that we rely on for our well-being.

We are delighted to collaborate with Dene artist and illustrator Cynthia Landry who brought the imagery to life, and Doris Camsell who provided the translations in Dene Zhahti.

We hope our work in co-developing resources like this one supports students in their own learning and connection to their communities, and contributes to language revitalization efforts.

JENNIFER CORRIERO

Executive Director,

TakingITGlobal & Connected North

Sį gots'ęh semo meʔeh Mızhéh Landry
gohéh nátthí hndeh. Ehdaro náhts'edéh.

My mom & I were living with her uncle
Michel Landry's family. We lived at big point.

K'ájeneh łúılı kų́ę́ godééla.

There were about nine homes in village.

9

Kíı ts'údąą húle lágodáát'į. Ts'údąą azhǫ́
Dene Xade kų́ę́ got'ę́ negodį́įzhah lǫ.

Seems there were no other children around.

All of the children were taken to the mission.

Łaǫlíh seʔeh Archıe Minoza
metsíe Paul Minoza ı́ųzhé
gots'ęh mets'éke gogáh aıt'įh.

Kúę́ godéla goʔóne
nımba zhıe nágendeh.

I spent lots of time with uncle Archie Minoza's
grandfather called Paul Minoza & his wife's home.

They lived in a tent at edge of village.

Łıe dzę Mek'eh Detę

Zaa k'eh k'amba gha míh datthíítłųh.

One day, he and I set net for ptarmigans, it being late October.

Meghǫnatthíít'e dlą́ą, nehtéa t'áh sekų́ę́
gots'ę́ nádehtłah. Ehtsíe kaséhndih,
"Ehtłǫ́ǫ́ sets'ę́ nadųtłah ǫhlée.

After we were done, I went to bed.

Grandma had told me "come back in the morning."

13

Ehtł'ǫ́ǫ́ k'ála godenítłeh ekúh,
Ehtsíe gots'ęh Ehtsų gokų́ę́
ts'ę́ náejíedetłah.

Next morning, in the dark, I dressed quickly and ran
over to grandpa and grandma's home.

Káá nełéhgíthe.
Tsıne satsǫ́ gáh
k'eekeh lıdí gedǫ.
Sı̨ zhu tsıne thııda.

They were up already.
They sat quietly, drinking tea beside the stove. I sat quiet too.

Káa łáat'áh gomba gołéh, Ehtsíe
sedenítluh gots'ęh míh ts'ę́ łedehtthííthe.

When it started to be a bit daylight, grandpa got

dressed and we went to check the net.

K'amba łié tthíí lúh. Ezhı k'ę́ę́ łié natthíí dlúh.

We caught one ptarmigan. Then we caught another one.

Mekų́ę́ gots'ę́ natthíítłeh
hıdı k'amba xąıch'uh.

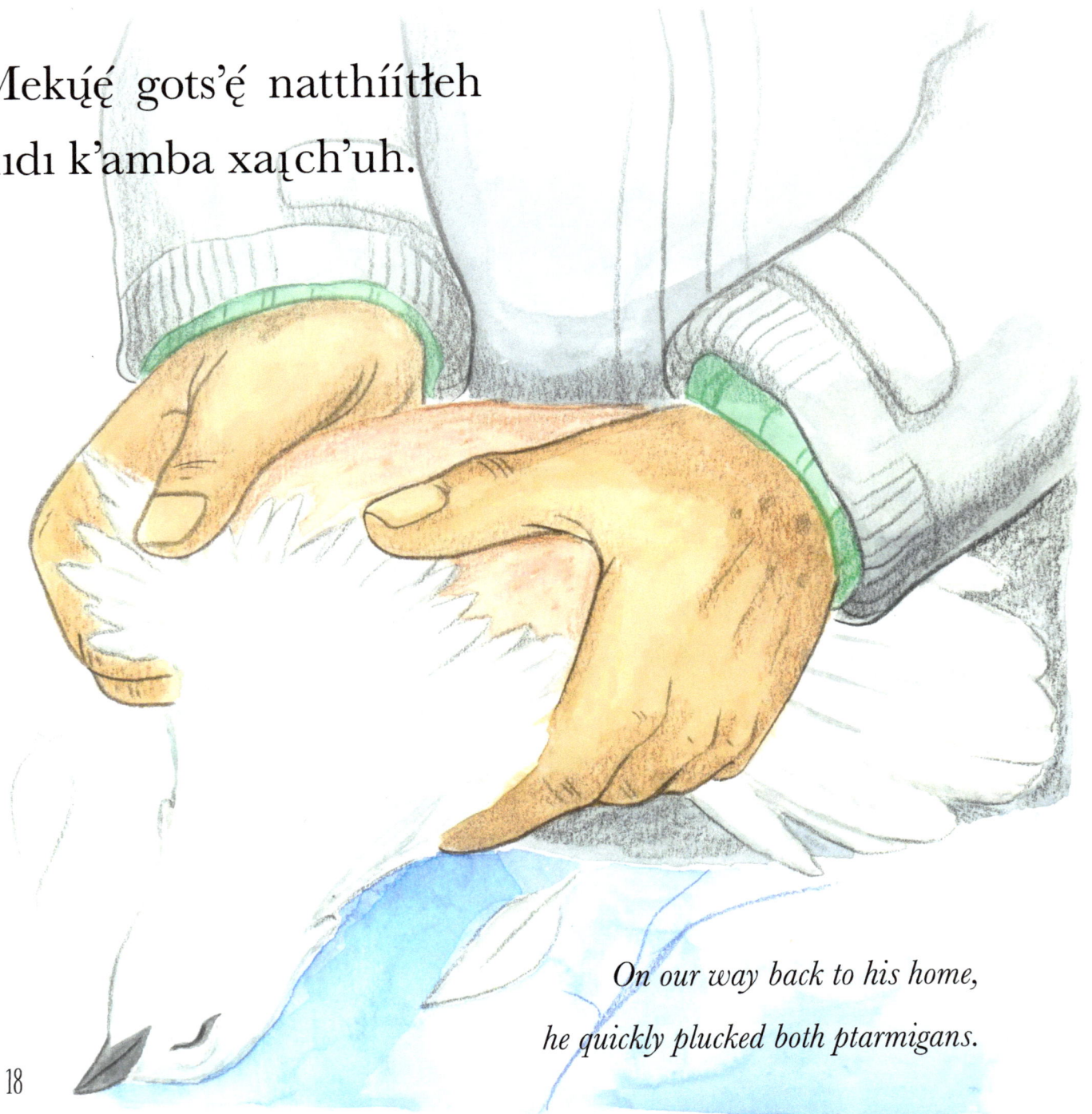

On our way back to his home,

he quickly plucked both ptarmigans.

18

Ezhı k'ę́ę́, Ehtsų ts'ę́ nezhue détthídhah.

ʔehgúdıh ahłah zhet'éh k'éonítheh.

K'íı tsíne gogáh tthııda gots'ęh náodeʔıh.

Then we brought them in to grandma. She started cooking

them right away. I just sat quietly by them and waited.

Tth'áh aetsílıa k'eh k'amba dzaa łıé níchúh gots'ęh senadah elıh k'eh nezhínıgéh.

Then on a small plate, she put on ptarmigan leg and placed it on spruce boughs in front of me.

Mozhéht'į kéoníhtheh.
Dįndée k'eh k'amba
goníh łekǫ.

I started eating.

It was the tastiest ptarmigan on this earth.

K'amba dzaa azhǫ́ mozhéettįh,
metth'ené zǫ dughaethendıh.

I ate all the ptarmigan leg except for the bones.

Dúh dzę gots'ę
k'ála menahndíh.

Máhsı.

This memory and relationship
stays with me to this day.

Mahsi.

Joachim was born on the banks of the mighty Dehcho (Mackenzie River) near Tsu Nahtleh, Fort Providence, Denendeh (NWT) with a Dene upbringing by being close to Elders. Attended Residential School for 13 years. Came home to Fort Providence at the age of 21 and as been on a quest to regain most of what he lost in language and culture. His biggest accomplishment was to stop drinking at 43 years old, and has been on a recovery and healing journey ever since.

He is an ernest student of the Deh Gah Gotie history. Picked up the drum in 2005 and has been learning Dene songs ever since.

Joachim and wife Nancy brought up 4 children and have since been giving back to their community, which they love dearly.

Mr. Bonnetrouge is still presently involved in community leadership and hopes and prays for a better tomorrow.

Mahsi

**JOACHIM PAUL
BONNETROUGE**

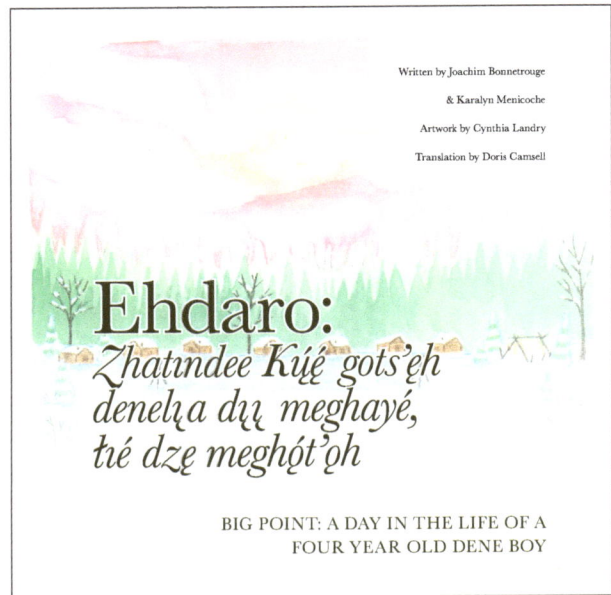

Written by Joachim Bonnetrouge

& Karalyn Menicoche

Artwork by Cynthia Landry

Translation by Doris Camsell

Ehdaro:
Zhatındee Kų́į́ę́ gots'ęh denełꞇa dų̨ꞇ meghayé, łıé dzę meghǫ́t'ǫh

BIG POINT: A DAY IN THE LIFE OF A
FOUR YEAR OLD DENE BOY

To listen to the audio book,

visit https://www.connectednorth.org/ehdaro

www.ingramcontent.com/pod-product-compliance
Lightning Source LLC
Chambersburg PA
CBHW042058040426
42447CB00003B/265

* 9 7 8 0 5 7 8 6 6 9 5 7 1 *